Davide Vasello

FOR A RESPONSIBLE ECONOMY

How to get out of the growth trap and put the
individuals back at the heart of the economic system
through a veritable revolution of consumption

Youcanprint *Self-Publishing*

Title | For a Responsible Economy
Author | Davide Vasello

ISBN | 978-88-92687-18-9

Youcanprint Self-Publishing
Via Roma, 73 - 73039 Tricase (LECCE) - Italy
www.youcanprint.it
info@youcanprint.it
Facebook: facebook.com/youcanprint.it
Twitter: twitter.com/youcanprintit

To my family

CONTENTS

INTRODUCTION

'It is the market...'

You have certainly heard this phrase, probably uttered in a self-exculpatory tone by certain entrepreneurs or politicians to justify the policies aimed at reducing rights.

Sometimes, it is said in a defeatist tone by those people who, while suffering the consequences of this economic system, end up resigning themselves to the idea that there are no alternatives.

The message of this sentence is: we should take the market as it is without trying to change its rules, but adjusting to it, even if this means a reduced protection of workers, the environment, consumers.

I believe, however, that the market is not immutable. We can change and improve it because **we are the market**[1].

Throughout this book, we are going to see how we can change the rules so that the market is no longer synonymous with avidity, which has gone so far as to trample on people's life, but becomes synonymous with **responsibility**. To make this possible, it is necessary to encourage businesses to become more socially responsible, since their activities

---

[1]   Becchetti L. (2012)

heavily affect the well-being of individuals as workers, consumers and users, as well as owners of the environment.

Businesses could be 'friends' of individuals and the environment if they no longer aimed to reap the maximum profit and if they added certain **ethical rules** to their work (Chapter 5 will explain the solutions in that regard).

The current international economic environment, however, is characterized by uncontrolled competition, based on quality and innovation on the one hand, but above all on cost reduction, for which the protection systems set up in the past are dismantled. In such a situation, countries tend to adopt policies in support of the competitiveness of domestic companies on world markets, thus renouncing higher standards of protection in favour of labour, the environment, and human health.

The fact that the economic system is based on competition is not necessarily bad since this may ensure efficiency and dynamism. The problem arises when competition is based only on cost and quality, while a third important factor is absent, which is **ethics**.

In the specific case, ethics refers to companies paying attention to adapt their work to the principles of honesty and fairness, while fully respecting the rights of workers, consumers, and the environment.

A company works in an ethical and responsible way when:

- pays its workers allowing them to have a decent life;
- respect the environment;
- produces good-quality goods and sells them at a fair price;
- pays a fair price to suppliers for raw materials, semi-finished products and parts.

Therefore, a company works in a socially responsible way when it does not aim at maximizing profits, but at a more **equitable distribution** of the wealth among the various actors involved in the production process. If competition were at the level of ethics and responsibility as well, individuals and their needs would be put back at the heart of the economic system.

However, we live in a **profit-oriented economy**, in which rules tend to favour businesses and, in particular, support their ambition to maximize profits. This is a flaw in the system. The goal of the highest profit does not go together with what should be the "natural" goal of the economy, which is to provide as many people as possible with an adequate standard of living, which is also **compliant with the protection of the environment and natural resources**.
Economic activities should be a **tool** to be used by individuals to pursue their goals; however, what happens today is that individuals are the tools to meet the needs of the production world.

The capitalist system certainly led to the increase in the standard of living in the past decades (with questionable procedures); however, it is no longer able to ensure widespread prosperity (the underlying reasons are explained in paragraphs 1.1-1.3 and in paragraph 9.3) and it is indeed evident that this system caused many failures in the current society: growing inequality and social disintegration, lower employment, temporary jobs, a more polluted environment, less healthy food, over-exploitation of energy resources and raw materials, environmental issues of global significance, etc.

So, how can we come out of this **wild capitalism** and achieve the goal of having an economic system oriented to ethics and responsibility?

A first solution would be to reform the rules of international trade in the direction of greater protection of individuals; as we know, these rules tend to favour the interests of businesses with the result that countries are forced to adapt their legislation (for example, flexibility of the labour market) in order to prevent other countries from compromising their competitiveness.

This solution, however, would require the support of many countries, which is very difficult to obtain since they want to defend their own interests and also because the position of large companies is very strong as they are interested in ensuring that the existing rules are not changed (unless in their favour).

A second solution, which I propose in this book, is **to encourage companies to compete at a level of ethics and responsibility as well**, and we are going to see how to achieve this by a 'revolution of consumption.'

List of topics.

The following topics are going to be discussed:
- the unfair redistribution of the wealth causing the problems of our economy and our society and the solution to come out of this situation: encouraging businesses to a more responsible behaviour;
- the fact that the working class, which disintegrated due to globalization, cannot expect a more ethical behaviour from companies;
- the increasing importance of consumers who, as a class, may successfully contrast with the economic and financial élite, thus recovering the social achievements of the past;
- the reasons why consumers may be considered ready to follow this path of social progress;
- the instruments that may be available to carry out their revolution;
- conscious consumption and how it can be an innovative form of democratic participation;
- the need for a 'one-off' relaunch of consumption for its subsequent redevelopment;

- the environmental and energy unsustainability of the current economy and the need for its simplification;
- the characteristics of the new economic model outlined in this book, the Responsible Economy, and the goals it may achieve.

CHAPTER 1

THE GROWTH TRAP AND THE UNSOLVED PROBLEM OF REDISTRIBUTION

1.1 The growth trap.

There are still people claiming that the redistribution of the wealth is a minor problem and the most important things are the economic growth and the increase in the amount of goods and services produced.

In electoral campaigns, the main objective declared by both right- and left-wing parties is the **growth** of GDP and the national wealth. Many people state that the economic growth offers the opportunity to ensure well-being without the need to impose sacrifices to those who have greater wealth.

For many years, therefore, it was decided that the problem of a more equitable **redistribution** of the wealth did not need to be addressed, with the idea, which has now become an illusion, that the 'cake' of the wealth (the famous GDP) could be increased unlimitedly and no one would miss its slice.

It happened that many Governments decided to not adopt more stringent redistributive policies, by partially draining resources from the wealthy classes to meet the needs of the most disadvantaged social classes.

According to the liberal recipe, rulers left the wealth largely in the hands of those who had achieved it, in the belief that it would be constantly re-invested in new production activities and would give new employment opportunities to those who had lost their jobs, while implementing an indirect redistribution of the existing wealth (I will talk about this more in detail in the next paragraph).

The belief that they could perpetuate this mechanism of reinvestment of the profits obtained in new production activities, according to the logic of continuous growth, led to an economy that expanded excessively, an elephantine economy that is thirsty for any resource and needs that everything that is produced is also consumed.

This resulted in the **consumerism** in which we are immersed, which has become a **form of redistribution** of the wealth, even when it turns out to be the purchase of useless or harmful products.

Therefore, when consumption is high, a larger amount of money is spent and is redistributed within the society. On the contrary, when the level of consumption is reduced, some of the companies are forced to stop production and lay off workers, with the result that unemployment increases and the national wealth decreases.

It is for this reason that **growth** can be considered a **trap**, as it makes **the level of employment depend on the level of consumption**, so that consuming large amounts of products becomes necessary to us, a real **social duty**.

Obviously, it is not possible to redistribute the wealth mainly through consumerism: it is a **perverted logic** which we should abandon. An economic system should be able to ensure a more efficient redistribution, while allowing everyone to have a decent life, without this depending on the level of consumption or the rate of economic growth.

Therefore, we should aim at an economic system maintaining adequate levels of employment without the need to produce and consume large quantities of goods and services.

This is possible only through a **greater redistribution of the wealth in favour of workers**.

In recent decades, however, it happened that a growing share of the wealth created by companies was taken by them in the form of profits, while the related share for workers decreased.

According to the 'Employment in Europe' study of the European Commission (2007), **labour income** in Italy declined **from 69.7%** of GDP in 1975 **to 53.3%** in 2000.

In the following part of this chapter, we are going to explain the different ways in which the wealth created by businesses could be redistributed and why some of these methods are better.

1.2 The different ways of redistribution of the wealth.

The redistribution of the value created by companies occurs in three ways:

A) in the first phase, with the payment of wages to workers;

B) in the second phase, with the taxation of business income by the Government, who uses those funds in redistribution policies;

C) in the third phase, with the reinvestment of profits achieved in new business activities.

A) The first type of redistribution is represented by the **payment of wages**.

In this first phase, it is difficult to have a satisfactory redistribution of the wealth.

The remuneration offered to workers is generally low because most entrepreneurs tend to keep most part of that value within the company in the form of profits.

However, if workers were paid with a higher remuneration per hour, for example by 20%, they could work for fewer hours and the number of employees would increase. This would be the ideal solution to the problem of unemployment.

B) If the redistribution of the wealth created by companies with the payment of wages to workers were not sufficient, a second way of redistribution would be possible: the **taxation** of business income and the consequent re-use of such funds in redistribution policies.

Theoretically, this second way of redistribution may be sufficient to rebalance those situations in which entrepreneurs keep a large part of the wealth created for themselves.

However, there are many difficulties in raising adequate funds by this taxation.

First, I refer to tax evasion and avoidance that, in our country, subtract tens of billions of euro per year to the government budget, which could be used for redistribution policies in favour of the weakest members of society.

In addition, it is necessary to deal with the current economic system characterized by the free movement of capital, in which companies have the opportunity to transfer their money where there are more favourable conditions, even with regards to taxation. So, in order to prevent domestic enterprises from escaping to countries in which they would find more profitable conditions, governments tend to meet their needs, on the one hand, by softening social legislation and, on the other one, by limiting taxation of business income. In Italy, for example, the IRES (corporate income tax) was equal to 37% in 2000 and has dropped to 24% since 1 January 2017 (as required by the 2017 stability law), but virtually anywhere in the world we have witnessed a decrease in taxation of this type of income.

C) If the wealth created by companies had not been sufficiently redistributed, in the first phase for the payment of too low wages, or in the second phase for the inability to raise the necessary funds for redistribution policies by taxation, a third way of redistribution would be the **reinvestment of profits in new business activities**.

Everything would seem to improve: the redistribution of the wealth taking place in the two previous phases in an insufficient way, would be implemented in this third phase, precisely with the reinvestment of profits in new production investments and the consequent recruitment of new workers.

However, the expansion of production activities is a phenomenon that should not be considered in a positive way only.

1.2.1 *Issues related to the continuous expansion of production activities.*

The process of economic growth brings benefits (represented by the increase in employment and living standards), especially at its early stages, but, during this process, problems will increasingly surpass benefits.

First, it would be necessary to address the problems arising from the **excessive use of** energy and mineral **resources**, as well as the high levels of **pollution** and difficulties in managing large quantities of waste.

In addition, the abnormal growth of production leads to **recurring crises of underconsumption**, as the level of consumption is unable to keep up with an increasingly abundant offer of products and services for various reasons.

In the first place, consumption is affected by the loss of purchasing power of workers, mainly due to the fact that the wealth tends to be in the hands of few people; in situations of economic uncertainty, moreover, even those who may be able to consume prefer to save resources for the future.

Finally, it must be considered that, in mature economies, a range of needs, whether they are essential or unnecessary, are met; for this reason, companies find it increasingly difficult to satisfy consumers, to the point that even massive investments in advertising and marketing strategies, aimed at increasing the attractiveness of products, may be insufficient.

1.2.2 *Factors that make the third way of redistribution less effective.*

This way of redistribution of the wealth must also deal with some factors that make it less effective.

The free movement of capital

The fact that there exists a system of **free movement of capital**, allows companies to reinvest their profits in countries that offer better conditions (cheap labour, lower taxes, etc.).

This means that, even if companies decided to reinvest their profits in Italy, they would be able to impose conditions: they could require the softening of social and environmental legislation, the preservation of low wages, high work hours, and greater job insecurity.

The fact that companies (especially the larger ones) may take advantage of the downward competition at a global level, while getting a greater share of the wealth produced, means that there is a loss of effectiveness of the redistribution carried out with the reuse of profits.

The liquidity trap

Companies do not reinvest automatically their profits in new business activities.

In situations of crisis, like the one we are living in, economic operators have **negative expectations** with regard to the profitability of an investment, so they prefer to hold money in the form of savings or for speculative purposes; zero or very low interest rates are not sufficient to encourage businesses to make investments because they fear they will not obtain positive returns from the potential investments.

Technological unemployment

Technological unemployment refers to the introduction of an innovation in the production process, which allows to reduce the amount of work used to produce a certain quantity of goods, instead of a reduction in the working time, resulting in a **reduction in the number of workers**.

Because of this phenomenon, new or existing business activities are unable to take over the remaining unemployed workers because productivity is so high that less and less labour is needed thanks to technology.

This results in a loss of effectiveness of the redistribution implemented with the reinvestment of profits in production activities (which should consist of the creation of new job opportunities). On the contrary, what we are witnessing is a tendential **negative balance** between jobs destroyed, due to the increase in productivity caused by new technologies, and jobs created in new production sectors.

1.3 Considerations.

As we have seen, the redistribution taking place in the second and third phases is problematic.

With regard to taxation of business income (resulting in the re-use of resources obtained in redistribution policies), we have, on the one hand, the problem of tax evasion and avoidance and, on the other one, the flight of capital to low-taxation countries.

As for the reinvestment of profits in new production activities, this leads to an enlarged economy, which can be positive in the early stages, but may cause more disadvantages than benefits in the long run.

It is, therefore, desirable that the redistribution of the wealth takes place in the first stage, so that there is no distortion of the economic system.

Companies, therefore, must be encouraged to further redistribute the value of production to other stakeholders (employees, consumers, and the environment).

It is right that those who manage entrepreneurial activities obtain a profit, but **the interest of the community** should be above all this. For this reason, it is important for businesses to change their way of working in the direction of greater **responsibility** and **ethics**, while better redistributing the value created.

CHAPTER 2

THE CLASS OF WORKERS AND GLOBALIZATION

2.1 Introduction.

In the previous chapter, it was said that, to put people at the heart of the economic system, companies should become more socially responsible, while redistributing the value created to the other stakeholders.

Obviously, it is difficult to think that businesses spontaneously change their way of working in the direction of greater responsibility and ethics. They should be encouraged to change their behaviour, and the only subjects that may succeed in this task are the citizens in their function as **consumers**.

This power to influence, however, no longer belongs to the working class, who, after a period of social achievements, has progressively weakened because of globalization.

In the following sections, we are going to focus on the working class, on its achievements and the reasons for its failure, and then on the reason why consumers, and not the workers, should push companies to adopt also ethical rules.

2.2 The class of workers.

A time of great progress of civilization was when workers realized they were part of a **class**.

Workers joined in organized forms and began to ask their employers for greater protection.

It was the starting point of a class struggle, which led to the achievement of the welfare state, by which workers are guaranteed a number of safeguards (pension, sickness leaves, maternity leaves, etc.). In Italy, the path of social progress culminated with the entry into force of the Workers' Charter (Statuto dei Lavoratori) in 1970.

Not many years after that historic achievement, the working class began to gradually weaken and the safeguards workers had obtained over many years of struggle were dismantled. The reason for this failure is the economic **globalization** and, in the next section, I am going to explain why.

2.3 Globalization as a cause of the failure of the working class.

First, it must be said that the processes of globalization, which date back to the Bretton Woods agreements, taking place at the end of World War II, have the main objective of promoting the development of trade through the dismantling of the policies adopted, rightly or wrongly, to protect domestic industries.

This objective was pursued in a first phase, mainly through the **reduction in custom tariffs**, agreed by the different countries in several decades of trade negotiations under the aegis of the **GATT** (General Agreement on Tariffs and Trade).

Later, in the 1990s, a specific institution was created, the **WTO** (World Trade Organization), which is a permanent forum where the different countries can make agreements and solve disputes regarding international trade.

GATT negotiations led to a substantial reduction in **tariff barriers** (customs duties), but with the creation of WTO, globalization policies improved significantly and affected not only duties, but also other aspects of the economic policies implemented by countries to protect their economies.

In particular, the **Technical Barriers to Trade**[2] (TBT) Agreement established that countries should not use the quality standards and regulations applied to products (the so-called technical barriers) for protectionist purposes, thus lowering the requirements to allow for the importation of goods.

With the removal of tariff barriers and less effective technical barriers, it became more and more difficult to prevent the importation of goods from companies that are engaged in **unfair competition** (taking advantage of labour and the environment). This led to a levelling down of protection levels implemented by the various countries in order not to lose competitiveness.

So, we entered the era of **globalization**, characterized by the free movement of goods, labour, and capital.

In the current economy, thanks to new technologies and modern communication and transport infrastructure, the production and commercial potential of a business has expanded dramatically; with its products, it can serve a spectrum of consumers in every corner of the globe.

The big multinational companies take advantage of this situation, which have every interest in seeing the removal of any type of barriers to trade in order to increase their production and turnover.

One of the phenomena that characterizes this era is the production **delocalization**, which may help us clarify how the new trade rules led to the defeat of the working class.

Delocalization is one of the biggest benefits that economic globalization offers to large companies, allowing them to set up their own production sites in the countries that provide greater return on

---

[2]   http://www.bankpedia.org/index.php/it/88-italian/b/18986-barriere-tecniche

investment, perhaps because there are lower labour costs, lower taxation of business income, and a less restrictive environmental legislation.

Large companies have a lot to gain from delocalization and their profits increase in a considerable way.

The losers are, undoubtedly, those workers belonging to delocalizing companies, who are left jobless overnight.

As for the workers of the country where the company delocalizes, they are typically paid a modest salary, so they get few benefits from the investment made by the company in their country.

The phenomenon of delocalization brings few benefits to consumers, who rarely see the decrease in price of the goods, which are now being produced at a much lower cost in other countries. Many people have happened to see, for example, a product sold at a high price and then they read on its label that it had been manufactured in one of those countries where labour is cheap.

Another negative aspect, finally, is the increase in pollution due to the fact that goods are to be transported over long distances.

It must be said that the profits made by companies may be reinvested in new business activities to further grow the economy but, as we saw in paragraph 1.2, the expansion of the economy is to be considered positively especially at its early stages, as the more an economy keeps growing the more drawbacks tend to outweigh benefits.

Apart from having inflicted deep wounds to the socio-economic fabric of industrialized countries, delocalization has allowed certain companies to expect more favourable laws from national governments in order to stay in their country of origin; in particular, for what concerns the labour market.

In developed countries, there was a **progressive weakening** of the class of workers resulting in the removal of the protections that had been obtained in the course of many years, up to the emergence of **job**

insecurity in the labour market, which meant the defeat of workers and of their expectations for improvement.

Globalization meant that the working class should no longer be considered only domestically, but globally, since there is a chance for the company to move to other countries where labour is at a lower cost. There are workers of industrialized countries who claim certain workplace protections, but there are also workers of developing countries who are willing to accept much more penalizing working conditions just to receive a salary.

This **downward competition** undermined the unity of the working class and then led to its failure.

If it seems impossible to rebuild the unity of the working class, we should pay attention on another class of subjects in order to stop the effects of this savage globalization and take a path of social progress.

CHAPTER 3

THE CLASS OF CONSUMERS AND THE CORPORATE SOCIAL RESPONSIBILITY.

3.1 The class of consumers.

Deregulation of markets was a terrific opportunity for companies, by which they could put themselves in a dominant position over workers.
In such way, the long process of social achievements carried out by the working class was abruptly interrupted.

Citizens today can recover this path, not as workers, but in their capacity as consumers.
Consumers have something that workers do not have, which put them in a favourable position over companies: they are the **necessary recipients** of the goods produced.
This means that companies can keep producing their products as long as consumers are willing to buy them (for this obvious reason, they should try to meet their needs in the best way possible).

In simple terms, this is a fundamental concept of Keynes's economic theory[3], according to which "demand creates supply".
Therefore, the demand for goods regulates the amounts produced and not vice versa, so much so that, when there is a shortage in terms of demand, that is when consumption is not able to soak up the entire

---

[3]   John Maynard Keynes was a British economist, father of macroeconomics, who contradicts the neoclassical view stating that demand creates supply, and not vice versa (he rejected Say's Law, as it is not obvious that what is produced will be certainly sold)
link: https://keynesblog.com/2013/04/03/occupazione-keynes-contro-i-neoclassici-for-dummies/

supply of products, the economic system is in difficulty, with the possible emergence of a crisis of underconsumption.

If the concept "demand creates supply" was affirmed by Keynes in a purely quantitative approach, I would like to consider the same concept from a **qualitative** point of view.

In this case, the assumption "demand creates supply" gives consumers an even more important role than the one of necessary recipients of the goods produced by companies.

This assumption, from a qualitative point of view, means that consumers are able, through their purchasing decisions, to influence companies to the point of "creating a business", not in the sense of its mere existence, but the way it operates and the type of products that it will have to produce[4].

This makes us think that, if consumers considered factors such as sustainability and ethics in purchasing operations, companies wanting to stay on the market should **adapt** their work to the renewed consumer demands, engaging in a more socially responsible conduct, which would result in greater protection of workers, consumers, and the environment.

Consumers have already some influence on companies and **their role is becoming increasingly important** in the current market. They are more demanding and careful in their purchasing decisions, including some aspects which they did not consider in the past.

This change in consumers' habits, which has occurred with the passing of years, has significantly affected the way businesses work, which increasingly make use of surveys or market research in order to learn about the potential appreciation of a product, or try to understand how to improve a good or service; not to mention the importance of marketing activities.

---

[4]   Zamagni S. (2013), p. 31

These tools, however, are used by companies in a reductive way. The focus is only on the usability and functionality that consumers may obtain, while appealing to purely individualistic aspects.

They rarely pay attention to the sustainability and ethics of the production process, believing that a more socially responsible behaviour goes against the maximization of profits, so these issues may be used by most companies in an instrumental way only to improve their image.

Ethics and responsibility may become the elements on which competitiveness is based only if consumers recognized them as important and, as **individuals who determine the market**, they should take the first step in this direction. If consumers gave importance to the ethical factor in their purchase decisions, businesses would have to adapt to their will to stay on the market and will be encouraged to behave more responsibly.

Consumers are essentially asked to gain **awareness** of being a **real class**, which, despite its lack of homogeneity, may be able to indicate the way in the current economy.

In short, there is a need for a **step change**. Although it is true that consumers are generally more careful and demanding, it cannot be said that this is enough to make them a class. It is important that they become aware of the importance of their role and of the fact that, through their purchasing decisions, they can influence companies in the sense of greater responsibility and ethics in the production process.

The aim is not just to obtain a strengthening of the consumers' position over companies, but to give life to a real **cultural revolution,** which puts individuals, and not profits, at the heart of the economic system, as happens nowadays.

In conclusion, we can say that consumption, which is now necessary for supporting the economic system, can become a valuable tool to transform it in the future.

3.2 Why consumers should take steps towards a better society.

While in the current globalized world businesses can choose the workers to whom they want to turn, the same does not generally apply to consumers. Companies aim to serve the largest number of consumers in order to increase their turnover, regardless of the particular characteristics of the consumers belonging to different markets. Therefore, if companies want to sell their products in a specific market, they must know the type of customers they are dealing with and take steps accordingly.

It must be said that companies are competing to obtain as large a slice of consumers as possible.

Obviously, it is important that governments adopt rules to counter monopolies and oligopolies, so that competitiveness among companies is genuine and may be based on the **ethical factor**.

The higher the level of **competition** among companies, the more likely these will adapt to consumers' needs for a more ethical behaviour.

In a market with a good level of competition, if a company did not intend to meet consumers' requirements, another one might decide to meet those needs.

An example will clarify this concept.

Assume that some of the companies producing biscuits use a harmful ingredient for the production process. Also assume that, as a result of a media awareness campaign, only few consumers are willing to buy biscuits obtained by this ingredient.

At this point, companies producing biscuits using the "controversial" ingredient have two alternatives:

- the first one is to drastically reduce (or stop) the production process, as many consumers now refuse to buy this product; in this case, their production quotas would be soaked up by the companies that produce biscuits with higher quality standards;
- the second one is that they accept to meet the new ethical requirements imposed by the market, thus adapting to the more responsible behaviour of the companies that do not use the harmful ingredient for the production process.

In both scenarios, consumers would achieve the goal to **change the supply** of the industry in question in the sense of greater ethicality of the products supplied.

This example helps us understand more clearly the meaning of the phrase discussed above ("demand creates supply").

For this to happen, it is necessary that consumers become aware of not being an aggregate of individuals, but a real class that, as such, can affect the way companies work in a decisive way.

3.3 CSR (Corporate Social Responsibility).

Corporate Social Responsibility refers to the attention that companies pay to the fact that their activity is not only based on the logic of profit, but is also marked by rules concerning ethics and considers the various aspects that are crucial to the well-being of the community. These aspects are basically three: protection of workers, protection of consumers, and environmental protection.

In order to be considered **socially responsible**, companies should:

- pay higher hourly wages to workers, making them work less;
- produce amounts of goods that are of higher quality, healthiness, and durability;
- reduce their environmental impact in terms of waste, emissions, amount of raw materials and energy resources used;
- pay a fair price to stock up on raw materials from suppliers;
- reach reduced profit levels.

Given the benefits provided to the community, it would be essential that such **virtuous businesses** had a strong presence in the market. Nowadays, only few businesses act responsibly and follow ethical rules in their work. The world economy is characterized by an increasingly fierce competition and companies focus on the classic factors of price and quality to achieve maximum satisfaction level.

Some companies manage to combine competitiveness and high ethical levels, but they are a small minority; those who try to operate in a socially responsible way and go against the "rules of the game", are facing higher costs than the "traditional" companies, and do not benefit from effective instruments to make consumers aware of their level of ethics.

To change the current competitive context, a solution may be a new "Bretton Woods" agreement, i.e. an agreement among the main countries to rewrite the economic rules globally, with regard to those on international trade. This solution, however, is not practical as it is difficult to reconcile countries that prefer to "make war" in order to try to be predominant.

Another solution could be a **progressive assumption of responsibility** in production activities, which does not aim to rewrite economic and commercial rules theoretically, but introduce the **ethical factor** in the competitive context with the aim that this becomes increasingly important up to the point of becoming a key component of the economic system.

Therefore, it is not about imposing new top-down rules, but **changing the foundations of competition among companies**, allowing individuals to control economic activities and the effects they produce on community.

Just think of the many important issues that are beyond our control and in which businesses are very interested: from increasing automation (causing a rise of so-called "technological" unemployment) to harmful substances in food, from the uncontrolled use of resources to the strong air, soil and water pollution. However, it would be desirable to enable consumers to have a say on these and other issues.

The next chapter will describe why consumers are **ready** to start the "revolution of consumption" immediately.

CHAPTER 4

CONSUMERS ARE READY

4.1 Changes in consumers' behaviour.

The function of the consumer has evolved significantly. In the past, consumers tended to accept in a passive way what was offered by manufacturers, while now they are certainly more thoughtful in their purchases, more sensitive to certain issues (quality of products and impact on the environment, workers, animals), attentive to the best value for money, less loyal to the brand, more informed and aware.

Such changes in the behaviour of consumers have been caused by the convergence of three phenomena:
- the loss of effectiveness of advertising, which today is struggling to gain increasingly disillusioned consumers;
- the decrease in the purchasing power, which has forced consumers to review their consumption habits;
- the emergence of the Internet as an environment from which to draw not biased information about products, which led to the lowering of information asymmetry between production and consumers.

4.1.1 *The loss of advertising effectiveness.*

The years in which advertising had more influence on Italian consumers were probably those of the famous "Carosello"[5], when millions of consumers anxiously waited for this television program,

---

[5] "Carosello" (Italian for "carousel") was an Italian television advertising show, broadcast on RAI from 1957 to 1977. (Translator's note)

represented by a sequence of commercials, so that they could go and buy the products they had seen on the television (the possession of which was considered a real status symbol).

Since then, advertising has lost effectiveness and consensus slowly, under the emergence of consumers who are increasingly **disillusioned** and less willing to trust the messages that are sent unilaterally by manufacturers.

Over the years, there have been fewer people who allow themselves to be influenced by commercials in their purchases, while there have been more people who feel a sort of discomfort for this constant bombardment of promotion messages, so much so that today tele-viewers tend to "escape" from advertising (the audience rating of any television program decrease dramatically while advertising is on the air[6]).

This loss of effectiveness on the television causes it to be more pervasive in other areas[7]. It is easy to come across advertisements wherever we go: we find them on giant billboards in the streets, on buses and trams, in railway stations. But the new frontier of advertising is undoubtedly the **Internet**; in almost all websites, there are banner ads, "pop-up" windows of sponsors, while videos are often preceded by an advertisement.

The increased pervasiveness of advertising and its impressive diffusion on the Internet are not able to change the existing trend; with the experience gained over many years, consumers have realized that advertised products and "anonymous" products are not so different in terms of quality and that the price difference may be due, in most cases, to the costs of advertising and the higher profit margin of the branded product.

---

[6]   http://www.digital-news.it/news.php?id=12380

[7]   Fabris G. (2010), p. 9

Consumers are much less willing to recognize the higher value of a product just because it is advertised. For the consumer to pay a much higher price for a branded product, it is necessary that this ensures a real level of high quality, with reference to the aspects of sustainability and ethics as well.

4.1.2 *The decrease in purchasing power.*

Another phenomenon that has led to increased awareness is the decrease in purchasing power due to the economic crisis, which has forced consumers to review their purchase behaviour in order to keep their standard of living, by adopting new life styles and consumption habits.

First, consumers are increasingly attentive to **prices** and the best value for money. This is shown by the growing success of the "private label" products, whose brand belongs to the distribution chain that sells them exclusively. It must be said that the need for many consumers to buy cheaper products, which are not often advertised, caused an acceleration of the loss of advertising effectiveness, which was described above.

Another phenomenon that has been taking place is that people tend to purchase mainly products "on offer" or "at a discounted price". **Sales promotions**, which are often used by traders in order to attract customers, encourage them to pay more attention to prices. In particular, these commercial operations mean that consumers become less "loyal" to the brand[8] and the company, as they are willing to repeatedly change in order to buy at the lowest price.

---

[8]   Fabris G. (2010), p. 236

In addition, there is a sharp reduction in impulse purchases. Today's consumers spend more time making their decision and thinking about functionality and attractiveness before putting the product in the shopping bag.

The amounts of products purchased are moderate. Consumers pay more attention to price, but it is equally true that some of them do not intend to give up quality and are willing to buy a smaller quantity of certain products provided that they are of higher quality.

4.1.3 *The advent of the Internet.*

The third phenomenon that has made consumers more prudent and will have an increasingly important role in the future for their emergence as crucial actors on the market, is the **Internet**.
Thanks to the Internet, consumers have the opportunity to get a much larger amount of information about goods and services, and this leads them to be more competent and aware in their purchases.
The network is now an environment from which to draw not biased information about products, which results in the lowering of **information asymmetry**[9] between production and consumers.

The advent of the Internet put an end to the era when manufacturing companies were the only ones to hold the information about their products, while consumers had to accept a small amount of biased information, mostly through an unceasing advertising bombardment.
Nowadays, there are several tools that are available on the Internet for consumers, so that they can increase their level of awareness and, consequently, their capacity for judgment and choice.

In this respect, a key role is played by the websites created to allow consumers to exchange information and opinions about products (info-commerce), in addition to online magazines and the myriad of associations for the protection of consumers.

However, the official websites of manufacturers receive marginal importance.

4.2 The emergence of new patterns of consumption.

In addition to what was explained above, other consumption habits have emerged in recent years.

In particular, this is what you may experience today:
- greater attention to the protection of the environment (for example, the market offers organic products, obtained without the use of synthetic chemicals, and products marked with labels that certify their environmental sustainability);
- greater attention to developing countries (there has been an increase in the sale of fair trade goods, which guarantee producers in developing countries a higher price than normal market systems);
- greater attention to the protection of animals: according to a Eurobarometer survey of March 2016 (Attitudes of EU citizens towards Animal Welfare), 47% of participants believe it is "very important" to protect farm animals;
- the diffusion of sharing economy: sharing means of transport (e.g. car-sharing, bike-sharing), living or work spaces, objects, clothes, knowledge and professionalism;
- the rediscovery of second-hand goods (especially at a digital level) and local fairs;

- the emergence of new distribution channels:
    o Discount stores
    o Maxi store (sporting goods, electronics, do-it-yourself products, etc.)
    o "On tap" product stores (mainly detergents)
    o G.A.S. (Gruppi di Acquisto Solidale, Italian for ethical purchasing groups)
    o Outlets
    o E-commerce

The emergence of new consumption habits shows that consumers are more aware of their role, but they still have to take steps forward. The new positive aspects of modern consumers are now necessary for protecting their interests, but it is important that consumers also become more responsible in order to complete this process of emancipation.

It is desirable that consumers become more and more aware of the importance of their purchasing decisions and the effects that this may have socially and environmentally. This will allow for the emergence of "virtuous" companies, whose work is also based on ethical rules, and the success of the "revolution of consumption".

4.3 The factors that hold back a more responsible behaviour by consumers.

It is commonplace to say that many consumers do not hesitate to buy the products of businesses that work in a questionable way at a social and environmental level, but I think that who say this does not consider certain factors that prevent consumers from adopting a more responsible behaviour in their purchases.

a) The first element is their **insufficient purchasing power**: many consumers would be likely to buy more ethical products if they had a greater spending capacity;

b) The second factor is the **irresponsibility** of a large part of manufacturers, who do not want consumers to pay attention to what is behind a product.

Consumers are asked to buy considering price and product quality only, and not equally important factors such as the levels of protection of workers, the environment, and consumers. A very different thing would be if consumers were **encouraged to buy with a critical attitude**, considering the effects of their purchasing decisions.

c) The third factor that hinders the assumption of responsibility by consumers is the **lack of transparency** with regard to the information about products.

The products we buy, in general, do not show how much companies protect workers and the environment, how they produce those goods and how many profits they obtain.

This lack of transparency means that consumers ignore the behaviour of companies and are unable to **distinguish** those that are doing well from those who behave badly.

Consequently, even when they are aware of the low ethical level of a company, they may decide to buy the product because they are not sure that competitors behave in a better way.

d) The fourth factor is the too high price **differences** between "responsible" and "conventional" products. If there is an excessive price difference between two products, especially when there is no adequate information to check if this is justifiable, many consumers may be tempted to buy the "less responsible" product sold at a lower price. If the price difference between two similar products were lower, consumers would be more likely to choose the more "responsible" product, as it bears a set of values that the other one does not "convey".

These four factors make consumers "less responsible", in the sense that they are offered satisfactory explanations that prevent them from buying products with a critical attitude.

The next chapter deals with the tools supporting the "revolution of consumption". We are going to see what solutions will allow us to overcome the obstacles I just mentioned.

CHAPTER 5

THE TOOLS FOR THE
"REVOLUTION OF CONSUMPTION"

5.1 Introduction.

This chapter will analyse the following tools in support of the "revolution of consumption":

- in the first section, I am going to explain CSR self-certification, which aims to provide consumers with the necessary information, so that they can make purchases with full knowledge of their impact;

- in the second to fifth sections, I am going to describe the solutions I propose in order to avoid the risk of a rise in prices due to corporate assumption of responsibility: indication of the level of profits, the knowability of the "overall supply chain margin" of products, the "step-by-step" self-certification, the reduction in VAT rates.

SECTION ONE

Self-certification of Corporate Social Responsibility

5.2 Self-certification of CSR (Corporate Social Responsibility).

When we buy a product, we know little or nothing of how it is manufactured and to which extent companies pay attention to the protection of workers, consumers, and the environment.

This type of information is rarely provided by commercials and the labels currently used, which mainly aim to **fascinate** consumers by showing the goodness and desirability of products.

It would be important, however, that consumers paid more attention to what is behind a product and its impact on society.

The first tool in support of the "revolution of consumption", the **self-certification of CSR levels**, goes precisely in the direction of making consumers **more critical**.

This instrument consists of a **label** that companies will have to apply to products by law and on which they will have to self-certify their levels of social responsibility; this allows consumers to know the degree of ethics of companies and, consequently, to **reward** those who behave more correctly.

The label of CSR self-certification would give consumers the unequivocal message that a product brings social and environmental implications with it, thus making people aware of the importance of their purchasing decisions.

<u>N.B.</u>: regarding products that are too small for the label of CSR self-certification to be applied, it should be placed on its price tag.

CSR self-certification will be related to three main aspects:
1) protection of workers;
2) protection of consumers;
3) protection of the environment.

In the following picture, we have an **example** of a label of CSR self-certification, with some "small balloons" that briefly describe the contents of each box.

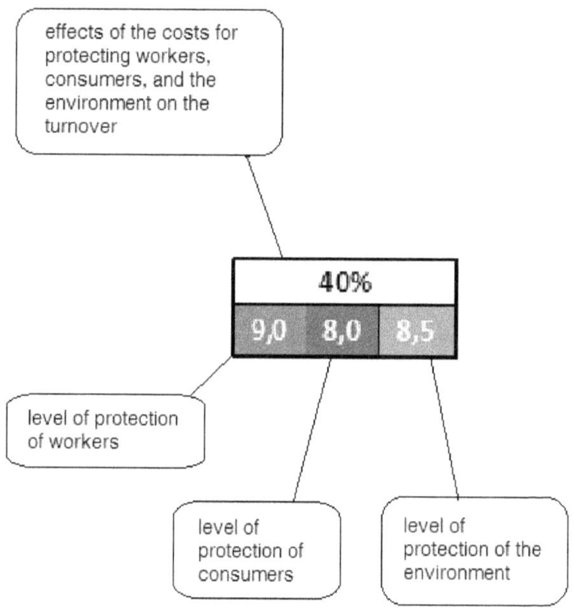

As you can see from the above image, a different colour is used to distinguish each of the three areas of self-certification:
- red for workers;
- blue for consumers;
- green for the environment.

5.2.1 *CSR levels.*

With reference to the label of CSR self-certification described in page 44, the lower line (9,0   8,0   8,5) includes the **self-assessment of the level of protection** of workers, consumers, and the environment.

These will be expressed with a number from "6.0" to "10.0" (approximated to decimals or to the whole number), while "SV" ('senza voto', i.e. without any score) will be used for scores below "6.0".

Companies will give themselves the scores for these self-assessments (the reasons why companies should give themselves the scores related to CSR levels are explained in paragraphs 5.5 and 5.6).

The companies will not be responsible for the reliability / congruity of the self-assessments of CSR levels appearing on the label, for which they will not be subject to any sanctions; the only one to which they could be subject is the **reputational sanction**, namely the loss of credibility and confidence when consumers notice any unreliable or inadequate information, which the company provides to justify the levels of CSR.

The **red box** indicates the level of protection of **workers**. This is determined by various factors: hourly wage, occupational health and safety, safeguards and services for workers.

The **blue box** indicates the level of protection of **consumers**. This is determined by the level of quality, product healthiness and safety, as well as the level of pre- and after-sale consumer assistance services.

This field also includes the ethical level of supplies: this means that raw materials, semi-finished products, and parts that the company takes in to produce the finished good, should not come from production processes in which labour and natural resources are exploited; this information also enables consumers to understand if the company pays a **fair price to its suppliers**. It is important that this aspect is considered so that consumers can get a **complete picture**.

It must be said that material purchasing for certain categories of companies (e.g. assembly companies) can be very important in the creation of value; if people did not consider this aspect, it would result in a distorted judgment with regard to the overall ethical level of a company.

The **green box** indicates the level of protection of the **environment**. A company that wants to work in a responsible manner should reduce harmful emissions as well as the amounts of energy, water, and materials used in the production process; moreover, it should produce, where possible, by using eco-friendly materials and design them so as to minimize the parts that cannot be recycled.
<u>This field also includes the level of protection of animals</u>.

The measurement of the levels of social responsibility associated with a product defines its degree of responsibility and ethics, so more or less "responsible" products can be differentiated on the basis of the levels of CSR expressed on the label.

5.2.2 *The level of economic commitment.*

The upper line (40%) of the label in page 44 describes the **level of economic commitment** to achieve the CSR levels; it is the sum of the costs incurred by the company, as a percentage of turnover, for the protection of workers, consumers, and the environment. <u>The costs incurred for supplies are not included in the economic investments</u>.

Unlike CSR self-assessments (whose levels can be set freely by the companies), this value must be necessarily based on objective figures. It will include, for example, security or personnel costs, quality control and environmental impact reduction costs, customer care costs, etc.

If it appears on the label, it makes social responsibility levels **more significant**; in particular, this information wants to give consumers the opportunity to reward those companies making greater efforts, in relation to the size of their turnover, to ensure the highest standards of protection. The objective is to consider the situations in which, to achieve similar levels of CSR, costs and related investments are very different; as businesses are different from each other in terms of size or type, it is inevitable that some of them need to make minor sacrifices to achieve certain ethical standards.

This depends primarily on the amount of turnover. Other determining factors are the following:
1) a strong mechanization and automation of the production process;
2) a high level of production outsourcing;
3) specific characteristics of the manufacturing sector to which the company belongs.

For example, a company with a high turnover will find it easier to increase the levels of protection than one with a low turnover; a business having a highly-automated production process or outsourcing much of the production (thus employing a relatively small number of workers in its production centre) will make less effort to give workers protection than a business which, on the contrary, have excessive labour costs in its production process.
Therefore, if companies are forced to provide information concerning not only the CSR levels, but also the related level of economic commitment, consumers are able to properly assess their reliability; in particular, they are enabled to reward the businesses that use more resources to raise their ethical standards.

5.3 Examples of labels of CSR self-certification - special cases.

Assume that two companies (Company A and Company B) have applied the following labels of CSR self-certification to their products:

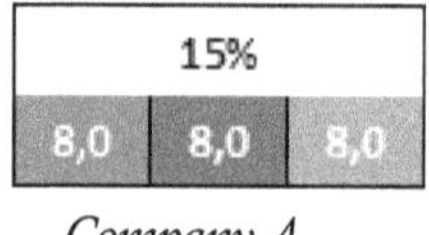

Company A   *Company B*

These labels have identical values with regard to CSR levels (8.0 – 8.0 – 8.0), while the economic commitment levels are very different.

While Company A spends 15% of its turnover to achieve CSR levels equal to "8.0", Company B makes a three-fold economic effort, spending 45% of its turnover for the same CSR levels.

Therefore, consumers will tend to reward Company B as they recognize its greater effort to raise the levels of social responsibility.

Sometimes the company gives itself insufficient scores (SV – Senza Voto) for the three areas of self-assessment, as shown below:

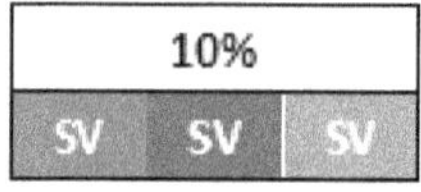

In this case, it is not obliged to comply with certain obligations of transparency (which will be discussed in paragraph 5.5).

5.4 The advantages of CSR self-certification.

The label of CSR self-certification summarizes the degree of corporate social responsibility with regard to three main aspects (workers, consumers, environment), thus ensuring that consumers have a **full picture** of companies' work.

The effectiveness of this tool lies in its simplicity, immediacy, and intuitiveness of the information provided, by which consumers are immediately able to get an idea of the level of social responsibility incorporated into a product.

Time is crucial because consumers' purchasing decisions generally take place in a short time frame; most consumers do not stop to read product labels as they do not think that the information contained in them is so important, and make their purchases hastily basing on the price factor.

The information on the product, therefore, should be easily understood by consumers so that they can readily become aware of the manufacturer's degree of responsibility and make the appropriate choices.

The self-certification tool makes businesses **give themselves a score** on CSR, thus triggering a mechanism of competition among them based on their level of ethics. The score has precisely the aim of **making** the different companies' activities **comparable** and allowing consumers to identify and reward those who have turned out to be able to achieve high standards of social and environmental responsibility.

This tool will also ensure companies a degree of **flexibility**, so that they will make the efforts they consider appropriate to gradually increase their sustainability, thus being able to plan the corrections that are necessary for the manufacturing process; everything will be left to the **free initiative** of companies and to their willingness / opportunity to join the new model of ethics-oriented competition.

It is clear that companies will have to deal with their impact on the environment and society, and many of them will be likely to take the "path of ethics" because they recognize that this is the winning strategy to be appreciated by consumers and gain market shares.

The fact that CSR levels are established by the company itself may certainly puzzle someone, and the following sections (5.5 and 5.6) will describe the reasons why it is believed that self-certification can give appropriate assurances with regard to the **reliability** of CSR levels contained on the label.

5.5 CSR self-certification and transparency.

How can the distrust of many consumers be overcome? They tend to think that companies pay attention to certain issues just for a publicity stunt. Their mistrust, however, is justified as corporate policies often result in something that does not match with the company's declarations of intent. Consumers can trust the information contained on the product, if there is such a level of transparency as to reassure them with regard to its **authenticity**.

Coming back to the self-certification tool, many may argue that, if companies could evaluate themselves about their level of ethics, then all of them would give themselves the highest scores. However, this is not likely to happen. Companies' self-assessments will not be based on an unrealistic view that they want to serve up, but on a series of information that they should publish by law; in this way, consumers could understand if the self-assessments about their CSR levels correspond to reality.

For example, a company could give itself higher scores than the real ones. Such behaviour, however, would be **counterproductive** because, in the absence of real information justifying those scores, consumers will neither trust it nor buy its products, while the company could face a serious **drop in reputation**.

A law will require a **minimum level of information** that companies will have to give on their website (by using documents and photo-video evidence) in order to justify the assessments about their levels of social responsibility, while they can choose to disclose additional information about their production policies.

With regard to the strategy to be adopted in order to increase their sustainability, and whether it has to be adopted, companies are completely autonomous and aware of the effects of their decisions in terms of **corporate reputation**.

The same law will not force companies to behave responsibly but, while requiring them to publish their CSR levels, will also make them **compete at an ethical level**, encouraging them to take steps to increase their levels of social responsibility. Companies that will not make their production process ethical, will risk not being competitive with those that do it and will be judged by consumers more positively.

Companies will need to give the information required by law, so that consumers can understand it easily and immediately in their control activities.

A free **portal** may be created where they can browse for self-certified products and on which companies can upload all information relating to their CSR levels (with a link to the manufacturer's website as well). In addition, to facilitate consumers' task, there could be also a **free application** for smartphones / tablets that gives CSR information for each product.

It was previously said that companies will not be responsible for the adequacy of the self-assessments; however, they will be responsible for the **authenticity of the information** required by law to appear on their website as a justification of such self-assessments.

In particular, here is what they will have to publish on their website:
- the amount of costs incurred for the protection of workers, consumers and the environment as a percentage of turnover;
- the level of profits achieved in the previous three years in absolute terms, as a percentage of turnover and in relation to the number of workers and work hours;
- the specific contractual type (fixed-term, permanent, etc.), as well as the level of hourly pay, for the different types of workers in the company;
- the measures taken to ensure work safety;
- the ingredients / materials used to obtain the product;
- the measures taken to reduce harmful emissions;
- the systems used to dispose of or recover production waste;
- the actions taken to increase product sustainability and eco-friendliness, as well as to protect animals, if any;
- the origin of supplies and their ethical level;
- the effects of the cost of supplies on production costs (these should not include the costs related to product promotion);
- the average factory price at which products are sold;
- a simplified balance sheet that shows the economic and financial situation of the company in a clear and simple way.

In this way, consumers will have some **points of reference**, on the basis of which they can better evaluate the authenticity of the companies' CSR self-certifications. If not, companies could provide some true elements, but of little significance and that only give a more positive image of what they actually are.

<u>NB:</u> those companies that will make insufficient self-certifications, by applying the label with the word "**SV**" (Senza voto – without any score) to their products, will not be required to give such mandatory information about CSR levels on their website.

5.6 Self-certification made by the company or by a third-party certification body?

In this section, we are going to see why CSR self-certification is to be preferred to a CSR certification made by third-party bodies, starting from the analysis of the **critical points** of a control system set up by a third-party authority.

1. A certification system of this kind could lead to a **passive** attitude on the part of consumers; knowing that a third-party authority establishes the levels of social responsibility, they might decide to trust, to a greater or lesser extent, the levels they see on the product without investigating what they correspond to.

    The presence of a body that reassures us about the ethical levels, would lead us to delegate it to control production activities. It is necessary to **get out of the logic of delegation**, and not to be content with a simple reassurance; we should control the ethical levels of companies' work ourselves, by using the tools that modern technology offers to us.

    Self-certification would encourage the **participation** of consumers, who would get information on the policies adopted by the various businesses and, probably, would reward those that will provide information in a more transparent way.

    What lends **credibility** to a certification or a self-certification is not the third-party position of the body making the assessments, but **transparency**, i.e. the opportunity for citizens to check that the CSR levels that appear on the label are true.

    This mechanism of citizens' direct control would be stimulated if companies gave themselves a score; if, on the contrary, the assessment of CSR levels came from an external body, citizens could decide to trust them and stop investigating the work of the company.

2. The CSR certification carried out by a third party represents a **cost** for the company.
   With regard to the costs of self-certifications, however, these are minimal because the company should just apply the label with its CSR self-assessments on the product and put some information on the Internet.

3. Another critical point is that some businesses may believe that the scores given by a certification body are not fair.
   The assessment of CSR levels carried out by a third party could lead to **conflicts** between companies and the certification body for the score assignment, with this resulting in real disputes.
   Some companies might feel that they were given a lower score or other companies received a higher score than they deserved.
   With the CSR self-certification system, on the contrary, this problem does not exist as the company gives itself the scores related its CSR levels and **the sole judge is the consumer**, who decides whether to trust the scores the company assigned to itself on the basis of mandatory (and optional) information.

4. The fact that producers may consider the scores assigned by a certifying body unfair, could lead to a **low level of participation** of the companies that want to submit to the certification activity.

If so, the impact of the certification activity would be very limited because only a minority of companies would start to take paths of responsibility and sustainability.

With the self-certification system, on the contrary, all businesses are forced to self-certify their CSR levels having to deal with their impact on society and the environment. Therefore, the positive effects on the community will be much stronger because almost all companies will introduce ethical and sustainability criteria in the management of production activities.

5. Businesses are **different** from each other in size, type and way of working, and then it is difficult that a third-party body can give homogeneous assessments considering the existing differences.

For example, for a large company, the investments aimed at increasing sustainability affect the turnover to a lesser extent, compared to a business with a reduced turnover.

The situation of a labour-intensive company is different from a capital-intensive one, which makes extensive use of machinery; it is clear that for the second type of company, having a relatively small number of workers, it's easier to give them more benefits without this impacting on production costs significantly. The same applies to a company that only assembles the parts manufactured in other companies compared to a business in which almost all the stages of processing are carried out at its site.

5.7 Effects on consumers and businesses.

Once it is fully operational, the instrument of CSR self-certification will bring changes in the modus operandi of consumers as well as of businesses.

With the CSR label on products, consumers will be encouraged to wonder what is behind a product. The goal is to **stimulate their attention** on the impacts of production activities, so that they might consider other aspects that seem to be of little importance. Governments and companies have been complicit in wanting an **indifferent** and **unaware** consumer. Following the introduction of the CSR self-certification system, however, the consumer will receive a higher amount of information, which will reduce the existing **information asymmetry**, which causes that a whole range of information regarding how a product is made, is for the exclusive use of businesses. In order to justify their CSR scores, these will give consumers the information that they refused to publish, thus contributing to their **consumption education**.

A change in consumer taste, in the sense of a strong preference for the products with high ethical levels, could lead to a **gradual change in the competitive context**: if the demand for responsible products increases, it is likely that there will be a supply adjustment with a growing number of companies that will operate in a socially responsible manner.

Therefore, they will be encouraged to adapt to the new consumers' needs, as those who first satisfy them will move to a position of advantage over the others.

The goal is to create competition not only in terms of cost and quality, but also at the ethical level, without the need for specific laws that force companies to protect workers, the environment, and consumers.

Companies will be interested in acting responsibly in order to stand out.

The introduction of the "ethical" factor in the competition among companies will act as an **antidote** that will make it possible to "heal" the current sick economic model. "Responsible" companies will replace the "irresponsible" ones, or will force these to act responsibly if they want to stay on the market with a leading role.

The most virtuous companies that will take the ethical path more strongly are likely to be rewarded by consumers and will thus increase their turnover and market shares. This will also encourage other companies to adapt and become more responsible in a **virtuous cycle** that will produce a real **renewal** of the unhealthy economic system.

5.8 Effects on foreign companies and domestic exporters.

A country can certainly force its companies to self-certify their ethical levels, but how should it deal with **foreign companies**?

Companies willing to export products to Italy may be required to apply the label of CSR self-certification to their products, which would have no costs: they should only stamp the label on the products and publish the information required by law (as listed in page 52) in their website, which is essential to show the reliability of the CSR self-assessments; it must be also remembered that they could also decide not to publish this information, by applying the product label with the word "SV" ('senza voto', without any score).

However, preventing the entry of foreign goods without a CSR self-certification label could be inconsistent with the Agreement on Technical Barriers to Trade (which was discussed in paragraph 2.3), which establishes that regulations and standards that are applied to products should not be used by countries for protectionist purposes. In such a case, foreign companies will be able to comply or not with the legislation on the CSR self-certification, so the absence of the relevant product label cannot be a reason to prevent its importation.

This does not mean that foreign companies will have the advantage of being able to operate without accounting for the ethical level of their behaviour.

It must be said that, if the "responsibility" factor took root in the Italian market, foreign companies should certainly adapt to new consumers' demands for higher levels of production ethics and sustainability; therefore, many foreign companies, in order to be appreciated by Italian consumers, could choose to self-certify their CSR levels and show that they operate in a responsible manner, even though this is not compulsory.

The problem of field control activities remains. In Italy, they would be carried out by a group of subjects (Local Health Services, Labour Inspectors, Finance and Environmental Police, consumer associations), while they might be more complicated to perform abroad, especially in those countries where there is less protection for the environment and workers.

In that case, the foreign company would have the task of reassuring consumers about the reliability of the CSR self-assessments, providing them with the largest number of information (being able to use the great potential of modern communications).

With regard to **domestic exporters**, the introduction of the ethical factor in the national market, by the mandatory CSR self-certifications, could produce different effects depending on the extent of their foreign sales.

As for the companies that export few products and essentially operate in the domestic market, if competitiveness were based also on the ability to achieve high standards of social responsibility, they would be encouraged to increase their CSR levels.

As for the export companies, they would find no advantage in increasing their CSR levels (this involves higher costs) if the consumers of the countries to which they export did not show any interest in ethical production activities; it is not certain that the efforts made to increase the CSR levels are rewarded by foreign consumers, who are directly involved at the level of consumer protection only. Therefore, for the exporting companies to find any advantage in raising their ethical standards, there should be a demand for more ethics on the part of importing countries' consumers; of course, this would be more easily achieved if, as a result of multilateral agreements, the legislation relating to self-certification of CSR levels were introduced in the countries to which the company exports its products.

5.9 Low-cost products in the new competitive ethics-oriented model.

As mentioned above, companies will be entitled to decide whether and how to increase their social responsibility levels. The fact remains that, in the long term, a strategy that goes in the direction of higher levels of ethics will become increasingly necessary for companies.

However, it could happen that some companies decide to increase their CSR levels in a slower way because they intend, for example, to produce **low-cost** goods and serve a public that has a low purchasing power.

Low-cost products, which have invaded many production sectors, from aviation to the field of food, are certainly popular in the consumer world, but can we consider them only in a positive way? This depends on the **cost components** on which companies act to reduce the sale price of products.

If a product has a lower price because the manufacturer invests little or nothing in marketing, sets a lower level of profits or makes a more efficient use of resources, then we can consider a low-cost product positively. In fact, waste, advertising and profit are elements that give products only a fictitious value and this implies that a reduction in price is not to the detriment of the quality of the products, with an actual increase in consumers' purchasing power.

However, if a product has a low price because labour wages are low, waste is not disposed of in a proper way and is dumped in a river, the materials used for the production process are of poor quality, we have to consider low-cost products in a negative way; in this case, there is a reduction in the product price and a decrease in its value, which is considered not only in an intrinsic sense, but also as the effect of the production of that good on the social and environmental system.

We can divide low-cost products into two types:

- "good" products, when price reduction is due to reducing the cost items that do not give any real value (such as waste, advertising and profit);

- "bad" products, when price reduction significantly affects factors such as labour, the environment, product quality, resulting in a decrease in well-being for the society as a whole.

In the new ethics-oriented model of competition among companies, "bad" low-cost products could be considered less desirable by some consumers. Once consumers will have more information about the real impact of these products on society and the environment, they won't consider them a good buy anymore.

5.10 CSR self-certification and advertising.

The information regarding the products that consumers use is little and often "partial", as it is provided by companies through advertising. In most cases, their messages aim to strike **consumers' imagination** rather than offer them the real information on the quality of products and their impact on society and the environment.

Through advertising campaigns, many companies exercise a **fascination** in relation to the quality of their products or their respect for the environment and workers. The contents of an advertisement can also exaggerate the virtues of a product or be so fanciful to the point of misleading the idea of the consumers about what they are going to buy. Through the advertising tool, companies may convey the best image of themselves without having to account for it.

Once the CSR self-certification system is in force, on the contrary, businesses will find it more difficult to give an idea that is better than what it actually is.

Consumers' purchasing decisions will not be based only on the limited and partial information provided through advertising, but on a whole series of information required by law as a justification of the scores that companies will give themselves about their levels of social responsibility. Indeed, if a company tried to give itself credits that it does not deserve, it may be penalized by consumers who would notice what the actual situation of the company is, may lose confidence in it and decide not to purchase its products.

When consumers have more information on products, they will make their purchasing decisions on a more rational basis and will no longer be the "target" of a certain marketing activity that aims to induce needs by leveraging emotional factors through repetitive advertising messages.

5.11 Assumption of responsibility by businesses and fear of a rise in prices.

A factor that could prevent consumers from wanting a more responsible behaviour by companies could be represented by the fear that "responsible" products, with higher levels of ethics, can be marketed at a higher price.

It must be said that **ethics is a value but also a cost**. Is it a value that will make our lives better or an extra cost that will be expensive for our pocket?

If we want the first of the two hypotheses to prevail, it is necessary that the additional costs incurred by companies to increase their levels of social responsibility will not affect the final price of products significantly; for this reason, such additional costs should be offset by a reduction in profit margins of the producer and the companies that distribute that product, as well as a reduction in taxes (paragraphs 5.12 to 5.15).

If profits lose their central role, there will be a positive introduction of **ethics** in the market, so that it can become a **third pillar** (along with price and quality) on which a healthy competition among companies could finally be based; their primary aim should not be to maximise profits, but their actions must be oriented to what Italian Constitution defines "**social utility**" in Article 41.

So, the risk that prices may increase if companies were required to be more responsible, would be avoided by the fact that the additional costs due to the increase in CSR levels would be soaked up by a reduction in profits and taxation. It must be also said that, in a system in which companies protect workers to a larger extent, they may obtain a higher purchasing power and choose goods with a higher added value.

What we essentially expect is not a reduction but rather an increase in social welfare, as a more responsible behaviour on the part of companies would entail greater redistribution of the corporate value in favour of workers, but also of the environment and consumers.

63

The second, third, fourth and fifth sections of this chapter will describe four possible solutions in order to avoid the risk of a rise in prices following the process of "assumption of responsibility" by companies:
-   requirement for manufacturers to indicate the level of profits achieved in relation to the hours of work and the number of workers;
-   knowability of the "overall supply chain margin" of products;
-   step-by-step CSR self-certification;
-   reduced VAT rates.

SECTION TWO

Transparency on the profits of manufacturers

5.12 Indication on the label of the level of profits in relation to the hours of work and the number of workers.

The previous paragraph described the fear that the increase in the costs incurred by companies to make their production more ethical, may result in an increase in the product prices. In order to avoid this risk, the first solution I propose is the requirement for manufacturers to indicate on the label the **level of profits** achieved in relation to the total annual hours of work and the number of workers.

This instrument aims to reduce product prices by lowering the level of profits.

By labelling the level of profits, businesses may be encouraged to **limit** them as they would be subject to the **judgment of consumers**; they may decide to buy and reward those businesses that content themselves with lower remuneration margins, and to penalize those companies that want to achieve too high profits.

Essentially, the level of profit will become one of the **parameters** on which consumers' choices will be based, so achieving high profits could be a **counterproductive strategy**. In order to meet consumers' **expectations** (a lower level of avidity), companies will tend to limit their profits to a level that will allow them to earn the fair amount, while considering the interests of all the parties involved in the process of wealth creation; in particular, the share of the wealth that remunerates shareholders should decrease, whereas the one in favour of workers, consumers and the environment should increase.

Why consumers want that companies do not achieve high profits is quite obvious. Profits are a part of the product price, which is a value for shareholders only, and not for consumers, who may be interested in the fact that a company produces a higher quality product, respects the environment or pays higher wages to its workers. Consumers normally focus on the real value of a product, while profits only give an unreal value.

Companies never boast of their level of profits although every entrepreneur claims that there is no harm in achieving higher profit margins as well. Obviously, no one wants to deny the positive role played by profit as an incentive to efficiency and productivity. It is right that the entrepreneur obtains a profit from his / her activities because he /she invests time, effort, and money, and takes a business risk, but the level of profits must be fair, **recognized** by consumers **as fair**.

Nowadays, however, there are companies that achieve high profits because they have established their name or may take advantage of dominant and privileged positions, while others are forced to content themselves with small market shares and lower profits.

When producers will be required to indicate their level of profits on product labels, the ones who have earned high profits will have to reduce them if they do not want to lose significant market shares. Once consumers are aware that the price difference between two products is not due to higher costs incurred by a company to produce higher quality goods, but simply to a higher remuneration margin, they will be unlikely to pay something extra just for a "name."

The labelling of the level of profits in relation to the hours of work and the number of workers, will be crucial to help consumers find the most ethics-oriented companies.

In the following example, we are going to see how to calculate the index in question.

Assume that the annual net profit is equal to € 4,000,000 and the total hours of work in a year are equal to 20,000 (10 workers working 2,000 hours a year each).

Relate the net profit to the total annual hours of work and the number of workers.

$$\frac{\text{net profit}}{\text{(total annual hours x no. workers)}} = \frac{4,000,000}{(20,000 \text{ x } 10)} = 20$$

In this case, the company has achieved net profits of €20 for every hour of work of each worker.

The following image shows how this index may appear on the label.

20

It could be marked by black characters on a yellow background and will be approximated to the whole number.

The level of profits used for the purposes of calculating this index may be increased by a major share of the costs incurred to promote products and to pay the members of the board of directors.

Transparency on product prices

5.13 Knowability of the overall supply chain margin of products.

Paragraph 5.5 shows that the mandatory information that companies should publish online includes the so-called "average factory price" at which products are sold. This information, together with the final sales price, will allow consumers to know the "**overall supply chain margin**" for each product (including logistics, transportation, and tax costs). By deducting the average factory price from the final sales price, consumers will be able to know the total margin per product retained by the various subjects of the supply chain and check its adequacy in relation to other products with similar characteristics and prices.

A better controllability of the price fixing process on the part of consumers, should limit the risk that products with higher levels of social responsibility are penalized, in terms of price, by a higher supply chain margin; consumers can also check whether a **fair price** has been paid to producers.

This may also limit the risk of a rise in prices, which could occur once the process of "assumption of responsibility" by businesses has effects in terms of greater redistribution of the wealth in favour of workers; essentially, as a result of this process, workers would perceive higher hourly wages with an increase in their **purchasing power,** which could be eroded by inflation in the absence of instruments curbing the rise in prices.

Price competition will not occur at the expense of workers' rights if the companies that work in the field of distribution **self-certify their levels of protection of workers** and indicate their level of economic commitment.

Within a context that supports for greater competition, also based on the ability to keep prices and profits low, a series of tax **benefits** could be adopted to reduce some costs that a company has to incur, even if it does not make any profits (IRAP (Italian regional tax on productive activity), contributions, advances, waste tax, etc.).

Tax reductions will be mainly in favour of distribution companies that have a lower turnover: this would be a solution to counter the "commercial desertification" (due to the ongoing economic crisis and distribution gigantism), which is making the socio-economic fabric of many cities poorer; obviously, fighting against tax evasion would be important, so that the companies that falsely report their income could not enjoy these benefits.

SECTION FOUR

Step-by step CSR Self-certification

5.14 Modularity of the obligation of self-certification.

The third solution to avoid the risk of a price increase following the process of "assumption of responsibility" by companies, is the so-called "**step-by-step self-certification**." It essentially includes:

- **step 1**, in which companies are required to self-certify their level of social responsibility with regard to workers;
- **step 2**, in which the CSR self-certification will be also required for the environment;
- **step 3**, in which the CSR self-certification will cover the three areas (employees, the environment, consumers).

Why should companies not be forced to immediately self-certify their CSR levels in the three areas?

First of all, it must be said that companies wishing to increase their CSR levels should also deal with an increase in production costs. The two previous paragraphs showed how these additional costs could be soaked up by a corresponding reduction in the profits that would be obtained by forcing businesses to offer greater transparency. It is difficult to say whether this reduction in profits will be sufficient to offset the higher costs incurred by companies to increase their CSR levels in the three areas. It would be probably enough if companies were required to increase their CSR levels first in one of the three areas only.

5.14.1 *Step 1.*

There are two reasons why it would be appropriate to start from the CSR self-certification with regard to workers.
The first one is that the main concern which need to be addressed today is to increase employment and workers' purchasing power.
The second reason is that, by increasing the protection of workers and allowing them to have a higher spending power, they can buy responsible products that promote a virtuous circle "light-heartedly".

In the first step, products will appear as follows.

This product includes:
- in the lower right corner, on a yellow background, the net profit in relation to the number of annual hours of work and the number of workers, which is equal to "20" (see page 66 for calculation methods);
- in the lower left corner, the self-certification of social responsibility for **workers,** which gives us two pieces of information:

- the level of protection, which is equal to "7.8";
- the economic commitment, as a percentage of turnover, in order to achieve that level of protection; in this case, the company invests 13% of its turnover to reach a level of protection of workers that is equal to "7.8".

5.14.2 *Step 2.*

In order to urgently give answers to issues such as global warming, the excessive consumption of energy and mineral resources, and the pollution of air, land, and water, the second area to be self-certified is the environment.

In the second step, products will appear as follows.

The level of net profits in relation to the number of hours of work and the number of workers is in the lower right corner (yellow background).

The **self-certification** of the levels of protection of workers and the environment, is in the lower left corner. We can see:

- **in the lower line**
    - the level of protection of workers (red background), equal to "8.2";
    - the level of protection of the environment (green background), equal to "7.5";
- **in the upper line**
    - the economic commitment, as a percentage of turnover, for the protection of workers and the environment, which is equal to"26%" (white background).

5.14.3 *Step 3.*

In the third step, companies will be required to self-certify their CSR levels also with regard to consumers (referring mainly to the quality of products).

They will be required to apply the complete label of CSR self-certification, therefore products will appear as follows.

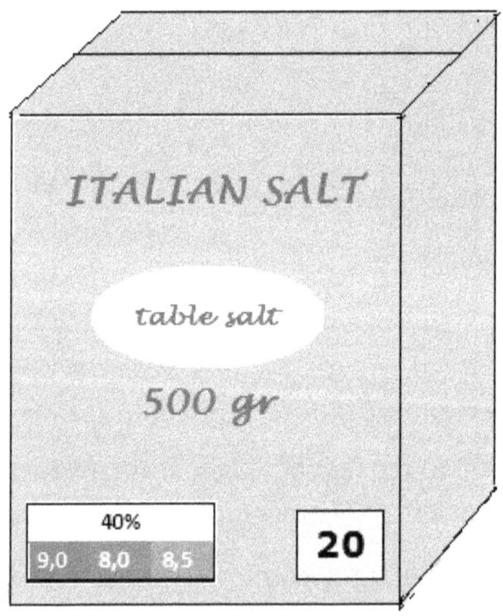

The level of net profits in relation to the number of hours of work and the number of workers is in the lower right corner (yellow background), which also in this case is equal to "20".

The **complete self-certification** of the CSR levels of protection is in the lower left corner:

- **in the lower line**
  - the level of protection of workers (red background), equal to "9.0";
  - the level of protection of consumers (blue background), equal to "8.0";
  - the level of protection of the environment (green background), equal to "8.5";
- **in the upper line**
  - the economic commitment, as a percentage of turnover, for the protection of workers, consumers and the environment, which is equal to "40%" (white background).

SECTION FIVE

The tax instrument

5.15 Reduction in VAT rates.

In order to control the price of responsible products, a **temporary lowering of VAT rates** could be provided.

The aim of this measure is to allow for a wider diffusion of responsible products, as well as a general relaunch of consumption, which is necessary for pulling the economy out of the current situation of stagnation, thus enabling companies to regain momentum (paragraph 7.1 will deal with a one-off relaunch of consumption). This measure would apply to products regardless of the self-certified CSR levels; however, the so-called disposable products will not have this benefit, as well as those whose production and commercialization involve considerable waste of materials and energy.

CHAPTER 6

CONSCIOUS CONSUMPTION

6.1 Introduction.

With the introduction of responsible products on the market, the understanding of consumption will change completely. It will be no longer considered a utilitarian fact only, which is required for satisfying a need or desire, but also as an **alternative way of doing politics**.

This chapter will show why **conscious consumption** may become a powerful tool in the hands of citizens to the point of influencing companies' work.

6.2 Consumption as a political act.

Political participation is expressed mainly by the votes of electors. Italian Constitution consider the act of voting so essential that it is defined as a right, but also as a civic duty. All citizens, therefore, are encouraged not to shirk the exercise of this important right / duty in order to contribute to a better functioning of public institutions.

There are also other forms of political participation: demonstration (certainly the most widely used one), petition, citizens' initiative and referendum.

Nowadays, new technologies help the active participation of citizens in political life by some tools such as social networks (Facebook, Twitter, etc.), websites, blogs, e-petitions, telematic surveys; many MPs are "online" and everyone has a mailbox to which to write in order to submit an issue or to make people know a position regarding a certain matter.

Certainly, for these forms of participation to be effective and produce significant results, many people need to be involved. Contrary to what one might expect, however, it happens that a good part of the population is not interested in public affairs: this is due to various reasons, which we are going to analyse through a comparison of the typical forms of political participation with the one represented by **conscious consumption**.

1) In support of the lack of political participation by citizens, it must be said that today's world is much more **complex** and this makes sure that many people struggle to get information and to develop an opinion on complex issues, while preferring to **delegate** without taking active part in the country's political life.
   The vote expressed at the moment of purchase, on the contrary, is more intuitive and simple, and gives the company the responsibility for how it contributes to the well-being of the community.
   It must be also said that the conscious consumption tool does not include the figure of the leader to whom we entrust our future: the process involves us and the product, which **conveys** a set of values, gives us information on its impact, and it is up to us to decide whether and to what extent to reward companies in the field of social responsibility[10].

2) Another reason for the lack of citizens' political participation is that many people believe that taking steps for a cause means wasting time.
   Conscious consumption would allow us to go beyond that bitter belief that everything is decided at higher levels and that we cannot do anything to change things practically. With this tool, every

---

[10]   Ceccarini L. (2008), p. 140

person "will vote" upon any purchase, thus causing a little **change** in society.

All products will be required to undergo CSR self-certification and consumers will choose those with either the highest or lowest scores; whatever choice they make, they will be **taking steps**, they will be taking responsibilities, in one direction or another, and then society will be no longer something out of their control.

3) Many people are also reluctant to participate more actively because they believe that politics can be a breeding ground for potential **conflicts**, as it entails a contrast of positions, values and interests that can endanger our relationships.

   With conscious consumption, however, there will be no conflicts to be managed; the only one may be an "**inner conflict**" between one's most individualistic part, which would opt for the less responsible yet cheaper product, and the most altruistic (but also far-sighted) one, which would opt for the responsible product.

   In the long run, dealing with this constant dilemma (every time they go shopping), and aware of the benefits that may lead to the community, consumers will choose responsibility.

4) It must be also said that institutions do not promote a more active **participation** by citizens. Citizens' requests are not sufficiently taken into account, whether they are demonstrations, petitions or initiatives; not to mention the questionable invitations to abstain (in order not to achieve a quorum) occurring on some referendums. The diffusion of responsible products on the market, however, promotes greater involvement by citizens. They will be given the opportunity to learn more about the impacts of different products on society and the environment, and then they will be encouraged to make a choice, which hopefully could be in favour of products with a high level of sustainability and ethics.

For these reasons, conscious consumption may be more effective than political vote when it comes to expressing the participatory potential of people, but this does not mean that it should discourage them from participating actively in traditional forms of politics. It is certainly good that most people take part in elections, proactive or consultative referendums are organized in the future, and the quorum for the abolitionist ones is lowered.

It is also true, however, that these traditional means of participation are not able to involve the majority of people or, where that is the case, it could happen that the votes expressed by them do not have a very high "quality" (quality means that they get sufficient information and have an opinion before they go and vote).

I believe that the best solution is to **integrate** the various forms of political participation that are available, both traditional and modern ones, with the innovative form of **conscious consumption**, which could get a large consensus thanks to its effectiveness and accessibility.

In particular, this tool pushes consumers to be interested in the impacts of production activities and this could be an **encouragement** for greater involvement in a country's political life.

Some people might argue that people have no intention to regard purchases as political acts, but I rather think that they can take due account of the impacts of their choices.

More and more people realize that they had been **dispossessed** of every political choice. Economic globalization processes, as well as integration among European countries, have meant that many decisions affecting citizens are no longer made at a local and national level, but in a supranational context by bodies that had not been elected democratically, resulting in a greater distance between politicians and citizens.

Many political decisions are **top-down**, while citizens' demands are ignored. This has caused the emergence of numerous committees and movements (in Italy: water common asset, No coal, No incinerator, etc.). This means that many people feel a great desire to regain control of their lives; for this reason, I believe that, if people are given the opportunity to "vote whit their wallets"[11], rewarding companies that act in a more responsible way, they will not let that go.

If citizens are able to seize the great opportunities offered by conscious consumption, they will go back to a **leading role**, thus affecting the economic and social context of their country.
Conscious consumption can become an extraordinary instrument of political participation because, rewarding the most responsible companies, consumers can **steer the market** towards a higher level of ethics, with obvious positive consequences for society.

If the market becomes more ethical, even the political action of governments can benefit from it, as it would be free from the strong pressures of large companies.
We know that **today's market controls politics**, which means that companies often set out rules. With the prime objective of maximizing profits and the value of their shares, they try to use any resources as much as possible up to trample on the rights of individuals, the environment, and animals, in some cases. Politicians often witness the arrogance perpetrated by certain companies without doing anything, if they are not their accomplices. However, if the market begins to change in the sense of greater responsibility under the pressure of consumers, politicians will have to deal with more "docile" companies, which will be less interested in pressing so that they make laws according to their needs.

---

[11]   Becchetti L. (2012), p. 127

6.3 Conscious consumption and its effects on businesses.

With the emergence of **conscious consumption** as an innovative form of democratic participation, there will be some changes in the way businesses work.

Being forced to self-assess their levels of social responsibility, they will be invited to **account for the impact they have on society with consumers**.

CSR self-certification does not force companies to behave in a responsible manner, but requires them to take responsibility for their own behaviour.

A company can also decide to work without ensuring high levels of protection, but then it should take responsibility for this with consumers, which could penalize it if they detected a lack of ethics in its work. The adoption of responsible behaviour by the company will not be mandatory, but will be necessary in order to avoid that it is crowded out by competitors, which will prove to be more responsible; this will happen in the actual, final competition, based not only on price and quality of products, but also on one aspect that has always been missing: ethics.

In particular, if consumers opt for products with a higher level of ethics, this will lead to a change in the supply, with a growing number of companies that, in order to adapt to the new consumers' needs, will gradually increase their levels of social responsibility.

A positive aspect of conscious consumption is that consumers will be pushed to be **curious**, to wonder whether the scores that companies give to themselves are true, and then to control their activity by modern technologies. The control carried out by consumers, combined with the one of consumer associations and government bodies (Local Health Service, Labour Inspectors, Finance and Environmental Polices), will ensure that any **differences** between companies' self-assessments and their actual situation will be swallowed up quickly enough, making it clear to businesses that the winning strategy will be **to not cheat**. Deceptive behaviour by the company, although it may bear fruit in the short term, would be losing in the long term.

If companies' self-assessments were not true, it would lose **credibility** and would be destined to succumb quickly, whereas the ones who act properly would be the winners of what might be called an **ethics-oriented competition**[12].

---

[12]   Hinna L. (2005), p. 110

CHAPTER 7

RELAUNCH AND REDEVELOPMENT OF CONSUMPTION

7.1 "One-off" relaunch of consumption.

The crisis has undoubtedly inflicted serious damage on many businesses. At present, only few of them could increase their levels of social responsibility.

In order to facilitate the assumption of responsibility by as many businesses as possible, even those in difficulty, it would be appropriate that this process starts **simultaneously with a relaunch of consumption.**

It might seem contradictory that we wish for a relaunch of consumption, as several parts of this book were about the need to go beyond the economic consumerism-based model. However, in this case, it would be a **one-off** relaunch of consumption, aimed to allow most companies to revive and use a more responsible behaviour.

Once the ethical factor spreads on the market, the consumption levels will be hopefully reduced because people's well-being will no longer depends strictly on these, but on a better redistribution of wealth.

We know that increased consumption would impact negatively on the environment in terms of pollution and higher use of resources. For this reason, it would be appropriate that the measures in favour of a relaunch of consumption are accompanied by others mitigating or cancelling the negative effects on the environment.

Here is a series of measures that could be adopted for this purpose:
- media campaigns inviting to moderating gas, electricity and water consumption;
- energy redevelopment of public and private buildings;
- priority to public transport and other more sustainable forms of transport (e.g. bicycles);
- encouraging the consumption of eco-friendly goods, as well as intangible goods and services;
- encouraging the re-use (e.g. "on tap" products) and limiting excessive packaging;
- promoting sharing-economy;
- encouraging recycling and discouraging waste incineration;
- making sure that the products that are expiring are sold at a discount price or distributed for free to the needy through non-profit organizations.

The need to ensure a sustainable relaunch in consumption has been covered so far; now, we are going to talk about how this can be supported by various actors.

Governments could adopt measures having positive effects on consumption levels, such as the transfer of the wealth from the richest classes, with a low propensity to consume, to the poorest ones, with a high propensity to consume: for example, cutting waste and privileges, using recovered resources in redistribution policies. Another governmental measure is a temporary reduction in VAT rates.

Companies (here we refer to the ones that are still able to generate substantial profits), may do the following in order to help consumers:
- paying higher wages to workers so that their purchasing power increases;
- commercializing products at a lower price.

Such a policy, which is contrary to the way of working that companies have used so far, would be totally in their interest: if there were a recovery of consumption, they would benefit from it with an increase in their turnover. This concept is summed up by a famous phrase by Henry Ford: "I pay my employees well enough so that they have the money to buy my cars."

Obviously, it is difficult to think that companies can voluntarily adopt such a behaviour; however, as we have seen, they could be pushed to further redistribute the wealth created if they were required to self-certify their levels of social responsibility and to publish their profit levels.

To relaunch consumption, **consumers** can also play a decisive role. In particular, the subjects towards whom it is more logical to claim expectations are medium-high consumers, who have an unexpressed purchasing power. They still have the opportunity to increase their consumption, but prefer not to do so because they want to save resources for future needs or they believe they are already content with their current level of consumption.

In these cases, the ethical factor may be one **reason more to buy**: the opportunity to affect society through consumption may be the right encouragement to push many medium-high consumers to increase spending even at this stage of stagnation, because it would be no longer linked to a need, but to the **desire to build a better society.**

It would be important to reach an **agreement between businesses and consumers**. This means that consumers should feel a change of course in the behaviour of businesses, which is no longer focused on profit maximization, but on **social welfare maximization**.

Consumers are willing to spend more if they have the belief that their money will not fund a failed economic system, but will contribute to build a different economic model, in which companies redistribute the wealth created.

Therefore, they might consider the consumption of responsible products a kind of "investment", whose remuneration is not represented by a certain profit margin, but by the improvement of life quality.

7.2 Redevelopment of consumption.

The recovery of consumption, therefore, must go hand in hand with its **redevelopment**.

This means that we must have products of better quality and with a stronger ethical content, while reducing the effects of those price components that only give products a fictitious value, such as profits and advertising costs.

It is more complicated to redevelop consumption in an economic crisis like the current one, but it is necessary because the current crisis derives from a wrong consumption model. Economy cannot be based on a consumption with an end in itself, the consumption of unnecessary products or that involve huge waste in terms of materials and energy used to obtain them. It is for this reason that a relaunch of consumption should be aimed not only to an economic recovery, but also to its **redesign**, so that we can proceed in a more solid and responsible way.

A redevelop of consumption is required to permanently change the direction of economy, to make sure that the same situation does not occur again after a few years. If it were solely intended to achieve a reduction in profit margins in order to lower prices, that would mean selling a higher number of goods, thus accelerating the excessive use of resources. On the contrary, we should aim at a higher **quality** of consumption, i.e. improving the quality and ethical values contained in each product.

If, on the one hand, it is necessary to increase the spending power by lowering profits and annuities, on the other hand it is necessary to ensure that these resources are directed to the purchase of responsible products: the only ones that support a **virtuous circle** and encourage a larger diffusion of the wealth created.

CHAPTER 8

UNSUSTAINABLE CONSUMERISM
AND THE NEED TO STREAMLINE THE ECONOMY

8.1 Unsustainable consumerism.

The neoliberal economic model, which is now prevailing, pays little attention to the redistribution of the wealth.

According to neoliberals, it is not important to redistribute the wealth in a fairer way but, in order to ensure widespread well-being, what matters is the economic growth, namely the increase in the number of products and services, as well as high levels of consumption, thanks to advertising and planned obsolescence.

Despite the GDP growth of the past decades, however, that economic model, which has not redistributed sufficiently the wealth but concentrated it in few hands, has proved to be unable to ensure everyone a decent life; in particular, the failure of that model is even more serious when one considers that it is **unsustainable** under several aspects.

First, we should consider unsustainability from the **environmental** point of view.

Production activities are having an impact on nature under various points of view: raw materials, polluting emissions, and waste. It is clear that the diffusion of production activities cannot be endless. The amount of raw materials that can be used is limited, as well as the amount of waste that can be disposed of, and the levels of pollution that may be produced without damaging the environment and individuals. If economic activities are continuously expanded, the impact on nature will increase to the point that this will be no longer able to support the economic system, which will break down inevitably.

Unsustainability also has to do with **energy**. The activation of a production process requires the use of a certain amount of energy. This means that a growing economy needs more and more energy and we know that, nowadays, the most important sources of energy (oil, gas, coal) are in short supply.

The decrease in the production of energy by fossil sources can be offset, by a rise in the use of renewable sources, greater energy efficiency and waste reduction but, if that were not enough to ensure the amount of energy required by the current hypertrophic economy, this would inevitably suffer a contraction.

The energy and environmental unsustainability of the neoliberal economic model makes it virtually impossible to maintain or increase current production levels, unless new revolutionary discoveries are introduced. Indeed, we expect a contraction of the economy caused by the lack of energy and mineral resources or the intolerable impact of production activities on individuals and the environment.

What is most worrying is that, if this contraction takes place within the current economic system, because of the way it is designed (poor redistribution of the wealth), it will produce a real collapse of the living conditions of individuals, which already suffer from the current crisis. It is therefore necessary to replace the current economic model, which is based on consumerism, with a new one in which the levels of well-being do not depend only on consumption levels.

8.2 Streamlining the economy.

The concept of streamlining does not refer only to quantity, but also to **quality**.

Streamlining means removing superfluous matter, while maintaining the core.

With reference to an economic system, streamlining means supporting the production activities that are useful for the well-being of citizens and reducing or eliminating the unnecessary ones.

In the previous paragraph, we talked about how the current consumerist economic model, which requires the production and consumption of an abnormal amount of goods, has led to an **oversized economy**, which requires too many resources and is unsustainable. With the rise of the ethical factor, it can be "**streamlined**" gradually and in a controlled way so that it can be more rational, does not waste any resources, pollute less, and produce less waste. Another benefit deriving from getting out of consumerism is the ability to put a **stop to commodification**, by making sure that some needs can be met according to some systems other than the market (self-production, mutual exchange)[13].

Streamlining the economy will be something inevitable and necessary, unless we find suitable solutions to the depletion of resources and to the impact of production activities on the environment and individuals, which becomes more and more worrying with the passing time.

Therefore, it would be important that companies changed their way of working in the direction of a higher level of sustainability, by reducing waste and the amount of materials and energy used in production processes, and by switching from the production of goods to the production of services, where possible.

As for consumers, it is fundamental that they choose the products that ensure the best ethical performance, possibly by reducing the consumption of less sustainable products. To this end, governments could discourage certain types of production with a significant impact in terms of resources. However, I believe that greater consumer

---

[13]   Pallante M. (2005), p. 25

awareness would be enough; once they are made aware of the impacts, they will understand what products they should give priority to in their purchases.

Obviously, the streamlining process could raise legitimate concerns regarding possible negative repercussions, especially in terms of employment, which may occur following the reduction in production activities that give people a job, irrespective of their usefulness or sustainability. However, the streamlining process will be made "painless" mainly thanks to those companies that choose to work in a more responsible way, and their ability to redistribute the wealth created more equitably, in favour of the other stakeholders, especially workers.

Responsible companies, in particular, ensure that workers **receive a higher hourly wage**, which results in a reduction in their working hours for the same remuneration. If the company makes its workers work less, it means that it will employ more people, thus creating new jobs.

Thus, we would go beyond the concern of a loss of jobs in less sustainable sectors; the creation of part-time jobs on the part of responsible companies would be the **ideal solution to increase employment** and make it possible to move away from the hellish logic of growth, which requires us to consume large amounts of goods in order to support production and employment.

This solution proves to be necessary if you consider that the processes of **automation, mechanization and computerization** allow for the production of goods and services with lower and lower demand for labour. Just think of the use of increasingly sophisticated machinery in factories, the automatic cash machines that are replacing cashiers in many supermarkets and motorway tolls, or the powerful computers that allow a certain amount of people to manage a higher amount of work.

As we know, technology aims to improve our life, but there is something wrong when its use has a negative impact on employment levels.

The problem is that companies are getting, in the form of profits, most of the benefits deriving from the application of technology to production processes. Technology allows companies to increase their productivity per worker dramatically, with a lowering of the product cost (due both to the rise in the quantity of goods produced and the personnel cut).

With the emergence of responsible businesses, however, a significant part of the benefits deriving from technology would go to workers in the form of a higher hourly wage; in this way, the introduction of new technologies in the production processes would reduce the number of hours of work, instead of causing the dismissal of some of the workers.

The **reduction in the hours of work**, along with an increase in hourly wages, can be the **key** to proceed with a "painless" reduction in the number of production activities.

CHAPTER 9

A RESPONSIBLE ECONOMY

9.1 The new model of responsible economy.

The new model described in the previous chapters could be called **Responsible Economy** or **Fair Economy**.

This model provides an **ethics-oriented competition** (or **fair competition**), which is not based on the cost and quality of products only. For a company to succeed in this context, it is no longer sufficient that it manufactures the best product at the lowest price, but it is important that it also stands out for the ethics and accountability of its activities. In particular, companies that want to succeed with this kind of competition will have to submit themselves to a virtuous path that goes in the direction of higher standards of protection of workers and the environment, while increasing the quality of its products and limiting profits.

9.2 The benefits of a responsible economy.

In the following sections, in order to understand the new model of responsible economy in detail, the main benefits that could arise from it will be analysed:

- **a higher level of protection of workers, consumers, and the environment;**
- **greater stability of the economic system;**
- **enhanced sustainability of the economic system;**
- **a more harmonious relationship among the various economies.**

9.2.1 *A higher level of protection of workers, consumers, and the environment.*

The first obvious benefit of a responsible economy, where companies are pushed to compete at an ethical level as well, derives from higher levels of protection of workers, consumers, and the environment.

A greater protection of workers could take the form of:
- an increase in employment;
- an increase in workers' hourly wage (possibly together with a reduction in hours of work);
- greater stability of labour relations (in a system in which working hours are lower, people can deal with production peaks with extra hours, while stabilizing a larger number of workers);
- an increase in liveability and safety of workplaces;
- greater compliance with the laws that protect workers (holidays, sick and maternity leaves, etc.);
- free business services (buses, canteens, nurseries, etc.).

A greater protection of the environment (and animals) may be obtained by the following actions:
- a reduction in pollutant emissions;
- a reduction in waste and a responsible management of them;
- the production of goods that are easily recyclable and eco-friendlier in order to minimize their impact on ecosystems;
- the adoption of farming methods that respect animals;
- the adoption of sustainable fishing methods;
- the self-production of energy from renewable sources.

A greater protection of consumers could be achieved by:
- a higher level of quality, health and safety of products (consumers' well-being would improve if they could buy products made with

the best raw materials, which contain no harmful substances and
for the production of which strict rules are adopted);
- a better pre-sale service, which gives consumers a whole range of
information in order to enable them to make the purchase in the
best possible way;
- a better after-sales service (an example could be the extension of
the warranty for durable products).

9.2.2 *Greater stability of the economic system.*

Given its characteristics, consumerism is **unstable** under different
points of view.

First of all, it tends to inflation as it is focused on profit: companies
want to maximize their profits and, given the existence of imperfect
competition on the markets, they **push up prices**, when possible, while
producing inflationary phenomena and endangering the stability of the
system.

It also tends to inflation for another reason: as it requires a lot of
resources, it accelerates their use, with the result that these become
insufficient and more expensive; the growth of prices for many goods is
now obvious.

The responsible economy, however, redistributes the wealth in a better
way and avoids unnecessary waste, so it ensures a certain level of well-
being with a lower use of resources. The decrease in the amount of
resources used in production would result in lowered inflationary
pressure on raw material prices, as well as in **greater geopolitical
stability** due to the absence of the need for large amounts of energy
and mineral resources.

Another cause of instability is that employment levels are **highly
dependent** on consumption levels; therefore, when there is a decrease

in consumption, there is a decrease in production and employment, with the possible onset of an economic downturn.

9.2.3 *Enhanced sustainability of the economic system.*

The need to maximize profits makes consumerism unstable and **unsustainable** both from an environmental point of view, for the devastating impacts on the ecosystem, and from an energy point of view, as it needs an excessive amount of resources compared to those that are physically available on the planet.

A responsible economy, however, gets out of the logic of growth, reduces waste and redistribute the wealth created in a more equitable way; this helps to ensure adequate living standards without the need to consume large quantities of goods, with less impact on the ecosystem and with a lower use of energy resources (which would be very important especially for the Italian economy, which depends on foreign countries for ¾ of its energy needs).

Here are some of the major actions in favour of sustainability that could be adopted by companies:
  - waste reduction, with an efficient use of the energy resources and raw materials used in production;
  - higher use of recycled raw materials, instead of virgin materials;
  - the production of goods that last longer and are easy to repair, thus stopping planned obsolescence.

9.2.4 *A more harmonious relationship among the various economies.*

In recent decades, there has been a sharp increase in productivity, which has saturated the domestic market of many advanced countries; it has become more and more necessary to export surplus goods and, to that end, adopt aggressive economic policies in order to increase product competitiveness.

This, however, undermines the harmonious coexistence among the different countries and leads to a "war of exportations" with the winners having a dominant position over the losers. This is even more the case when this "war" is among the countries belonging to the same monetary zone, which agreed to deprive themselves of currency depreciation, which allows those in need to recover competitiveness by making exports cheaper.

An example of this is precisely Europe: the adoption of a single currency on the part of countries having very different rates of competition, has led to a situation in which the trade surplus of Northern Europe countries (Germany at the top) coincided with the trade deficits of the so-called PIIGS[14] (Portugal, Italy, Ireland, Greece, Spain), which contributed to the debt of these countries at both public and private levels.

Obviously, a competitive model that leads to a situation in which some countries tend to dominate over the others cannot work. It may lead to tensions and also conflicts, not to mention the suffering of the people living in those countries losing the competition.

A responsible economy, on the contrary, favours harmony in the relations among countries. Aiming to streamline economies, it limits the risk of market saturation, which pushes countries to the obsessive search for exports to the detriment of the others; therefore, the well-

---

[14]   Bagnai A. (2012), p. 54

being of a population does not depend on the exporting capacity of the country, but it is guaranteed by an efficient use of resources.

A streamlined economy, moreover, needs a lower amount of energy and mineral resources to work and this results in **greater geopolitical stability**.

All this would go towards the end of the existing global "economic war", due less to the single countries wanting to offer better living conditions than their desire to give large businesses the maximum benefits offered by globalization. The goal on which we must focus is to make economies more self-sufficient by a process of "**deglobalization**" limiting commercial exchanges to advantageous products only.

In this sense, a system of self-certification of companies' social responsibility levels can be useful for self-regulating trade. Consumers, will have a preference for domestic products, so that the money they spend to buy responsible companies' goods benefits the community to which they belong; this will lead to the replacement of state protectionism with a "widespread protection" on the part of citizens.

The current lack of harmony in the relations among the various economies is even more evident when reference is made to the economic relations with the **South of the world**. These countries are pushed by their needs (if they are not ruled by corrupt governments), so they are forced to trade their resources at low prices, which are not enough to allow their populations to enjoy decent living conditions.

CSR self-certification can be a possible solution to this problem: if they are required to provide information on their **ethical level of supply**, companies are encouraged to pay a fair price for importing goods, provided that they are not from places where workers and the environment are exploited; otherwise, consumers may choose to refrain from buying their products.

A higher ethical level in trade will allow developing countries to have the resources that are necessary for creating a situation of greater prosperity for their populations, so that they are no longer forced to leave their country to seek their fortune in advanced countries.

9.3 The responsible economy and the "visible hand".

Many know the metaphor of the "invisible hand", according to which the market works in such a way as to allow that the selfish search for personal interest leads to the welfare of society.

According to this vision of the economy, therefore, it is not necessary to redistribute the wealth created more equitably, but to focus on growth in the belief that, if you let the economic agents maximize their own profits, this will give the community some benefits.

This system, however, has proven to work up to a certain point. The growth of an economy has to be considered positively, in particular at its early stages, in which it is necessary to raise the standard of living, there are many needs to be met, there are many resources available, the level of production is not likely to have significant adverse effects on the environment and individuals, and the phenomenon of technological unemployment can still be kept at bay by the emergence of employment opportunities in new sectors.

However, in a mature economy, in the absence of the aforementioned conditions, it is wrong to pursue the objective of a further increase in production; on the contrary, one should try to redistribute the wealth more equally and to redevelop production activities.

In light of the issues related to the continuous growth of production, there is an unfounded belief, which is that self-interest would allow economic balance through market automatisms (the so-called "invisible hand"). For the economic system to work at its best, however, it is necessary that businesses and consumers take due account of the impact of their behaviour and that their choices are not merely the result of a self-interest, but also a form of **far-sighted altruism**.

As opposed to the "invisible hand", which operates involuntarily in an attempt to reconcile the individual self-interests with collective well-being, we may define "**visible hand**", which rather works in a **voluntary** way, the adoption of a more responsible and ethical behaviour by economic agents. In this case, the benefits for the community are not the result of uncontrolled market forces operating in a disordered way, but of an explicit desire of businesses and consumers to spread the wealth through their choices.
In particular, if consumers give priority to more responsible products in their purchases and businesses adapt to renewed demand requirements, this will result in greater protection of workers, consumers, and the environment.

As mentioned in the introduction to this book, the market is not an immutable entity. We can change the way it works so that there is a **mediation** between the self-interest of economic agents and their more responsible and altruist behaviour.

CHAPTER 10

CONCLUSIONS

In conclusion, we can say that, with the advent of the Responsible Economy, companies are asked to take responsibility and ensure that their work is not based on a mere economic self-interest. The ultimate goal is to ensure that competition among companies is also based on ethics and that their primary objective is not to maximize profits, but to maximize social well-being.

With regard to consumers, it is hoped that many of them make their purchasing decisions not only according to individualistic criteria related to the satisfaction of their needs, but also considering public interests, which is basically one's own interest too. Through a conscious and responsible form of consumption, they can decide where the economic system will go and what values have to be protected (work, product quality, the environment), by giving their own contribution for a better world.

Benefits would not be at an economic level only, but above all at a personal one, with a significant improvement in quality of life and relationships.

If a responsible economy gains ground, we will be able to put individuals at the heart of the economic system and to get out of the disastrous neoliberal model based on an outdated indicator like GDP, which, as stated by Robert Kennedy in one of his famous speeches, "measures everything except that which makes life worthwhile".

BIBLIOGRAPHY

Bagnai A. (2012) - *Il tramonto dell'euro. Come e perché la fine della moneta unica salverebbe democrazia e benessere in Europa* - Imprimatur, Reggio-Emilia

Becchetti L. (2012) - *Il mercato siamo noi* - Bruno Mondadori, Milano

Bhagwati J. (2004) – *In Defense of Globalization* – Oxford University Press, Oxford; trad. (2005) *Elogio della globalizzazione* - Laterza, Roma-Bari

Bologna G. (2005) - *Manuale della sostenibilità : idee, concetti, nuove discipline capaci di futuro* - Edizioni Ambiente, Milano

Ceccarini L. (2008) - *Consumare con impegno* - Laterza, Roma-Bari

Daly H. (1977) – *Steady-state economics. The political economy of bio-physical equilibrium and moral growth* – W. H. Freeman and Co., San Francisco; trad. (1981) *Lo stato stazionario : l'economia dell'equilibrio biofisico e della crescita morale* - Sansoni, Firenze

Fabris G. (2010) - *La società post-crescita. Consumi e stili di vita* - Egea, Milano

Hinna L. (2005) - *Gli impatti organizzativi e gestionali dell'orientamento alla CSR delle aziende* in Paltrinieri R, Parmigiani M.L. (a cura di), *Sostenibilità ed etica* - Carocci Editore, Roma

Mongardini C. (2007) - *Capitalismo e politica nell'era della globalizzazione* - Franco Angeli, Milano

Pallante M. (2005) - *La decrescita felice. La qualità della vita non dipende dal PIL* - Editori Riuniti, Roma

Rifkin J. (1995) – *The End of Work: The Decline of the Global Labor Force and the Dawn of the Post-Market Era* – G. P. Putnam's Sons, New York; trad. (1995) *La fine del lavoro. Il declino della forza lavoro globale e l'avvento dell'era post-mercato* - Baldini & Castoldi, Milano

Rifkin J. (2002) – *The Hydrogen Economy* – Putnam-Tarcher, New York; trad. (2002) *Economia all'idrogeno* – A. Mondadori, Milano

Rifkin J. (2009) – *The Empathic Civilization: The Race to Global Consciousness in a World in Crisis* – Tarcher-Penguin, New York; trad. (2010) *La civiltà dell'empatia. La corsa verso la coscienza globale nel mondo in crisi* - A. Mondadori, Milano

Stiglitz J. (2002) – *Globalization and its discontents* – Penguin Books, London; trad. (2002) *La globalizzazione e i suoi oppositori* - Einaudi, Torino

Stiglitz J. (2006) – *Making globalization work* – W. W. Norton & Co., New York; trad. (2006) *La globalizzazione che funziona* - Einaudi, Torino

Tiezzi E., Marchettini N. (1999) - *Che cos'è lo sviluppo sostenibile? : le basi scientifiche della sostenibilita e i guasti del pensiero unico* - Donzelli, Roma

Villani A. (2001) - *Gli economisti, la distribuzione, la giustizia: Friedrich von Hayek, John Maynard Keynes, Milton Friedman* - I.S.U. Università Cattolica, Milano

Wolf M. (2004) – *Why Globalization Works* – Yale University Press, New Haven; trad. (2006) *Perché la globalizzazione funziona* - Il Mulino, Bologna

Zamagni S. (2013) - *Impresa responsabile e mercato civile* - Il Mulino, Bologna

Printed in October 2017 by
Youcanprint *Self-Publishing*